LARGE PRI
JOKES

Compiled by Hugh Morrison

Montpelier Publishing
London
MMXV

ISBN-13: 978-1517775780
ISBN-10: 1517775787
Published by Montpelier Publishing, London.
Printed by Amazon Createspace.

A fat man wanted to lose weight so he went to the doctor who made him stand on the scales. The man sucked his tummy in. 'That won't help you,' said the doctor. 'Yes it will,' said the man, 'I can see the numbers now.'

Husband: Darling, will you still love me when I'm old, fat and balding?
Wife: I do.

A hysterical woman burst into the office of a hypnotherapist. 'Doctor, you must help me!' she cried. 'I've been faithful to my husband for twenty five years, but last night I slept with a complete stranger. I feel so guilty – you must hypnotise me so that I forget all about it!'
The doctor sighed and said 'not you again...'

'Why did you dump your girlfriend?'
'She kept using four letter words.'
'Is that so bad?'
'It is if they're words like "stop,", "don't", "can't", and "won't".'

'There's nothing really wrong with you,' said the doctor to his patient. 'Just drink a glass of this tonic each night followed by a hot bath and you'll be right as rain.'
The next day the doctor returned to check on the man who looked worse than ever.

'Did you drink the tonic?' asked the doctor.
'Yes,' said the man, 'but I could only manage half the hot bath.'

My wife and I celebrated our tenth wedding anniversary by going back to the hotel we spent our honeymoon night in. Only this time, it was me who stayed in the bathroom and cried!

Doctor: There's nothing wrong with you. You'll live to be sixty.
Patient: I AM sixty!
Doctor: See, what did I tell you!

Farmer Giles wanted to buy his neighbour's cow, but on enquiring the price he was shocked to learn it was £50.
'What', he protested, 'here I am, your friend and neighbour, and you ask a price like that?'
'I'll tell you what', replied the other farmer, 'seeing you are my neighbour I'll give you 20% discount.'
Now Farmer Giles was not much of a scholar and he wasn't quite sure what this meant so he said 'I'll think about it.'
He went off down the road and was still trying to figure it out when he saw the local school-mistress coming towards him on her bicycle. He beckoned her to stop and said
'Now tell me, Miss Smith, if I were to offer you £50, less 20% discount, what would you take off?'
Miss Smith thought for a moment and then declared 'Everything, except my ear-rings.'

'Have you ever had an ex-girlfriend you can't get rid of?'
'Yes – my wife.'

Sir Winston Churchill is said to have attended a banquet where he sat next to a Methodist minister with strict views on temperance. A waitress offered Sir Winston a glass of wine, who took one, and then moved on to the minister. 'Young lady,' said the clergyman in a shocked voice, 'I would rather commit adultery than drink alcohol.' Sir Winston called to the waitress, 'Come back - I didn't realise there was a choice!'

Smith: How did you get on at the doctor?
Jones: Bad news I'm afraid. I've got to take a tablet every day for the rest of my life.
Smith: That doesn't sound too bad, what are you worried about?
Jones: He only gave me three tablets!

'I'll never forget the day of my wife's funeral. There was a huge crowd and we sang 'Abide with Me'.
'It sounds like a lovely service.'
'Oh, I didn't go to the service, it was Cup Final day.'

'Doctor, I'm thinking of getting a vasectomy.'
'That's a big decision. Have you discussed it with your family?'
'Yes, we took a vote, and they're in favour of it 15 to 2.'

Patient: I keep dreaming that beautiful women are throwing themselves at me, but that I keep pushing them away.
Doctor: Well, what do you want me to do about it?
Patient: Break my arm.

An American tourist arrived at Heathrow and got into a taxi. Just outside the airport the taxi stopped at a Pelican crossing. The tourist heard the sound of the crossing signal and asked the driver, 'hey buddy, what's that beeping noise?'
'That's so that blind people know when the lights are green,' said the driver.
'My God,' cried the American. 'You mean they let blind people drive here?'

An alcoholic, a compulsive eater and a hypochondriac were sitting in a doctor's waiting room.
'I'm so tired and thirsty, I must have a glass of whisky,' said the alcoholic.
'I'm so tired and thirsty, I must have a double milk shake,' said the compulsive eater.
'I'm so tired and thirsty,' said the hypochondriac, 'I must have diabetes.'

Magistrate (to defendant): You've been brought here for drinking.
Defendant: OK, then let's get started!

What's the easiest way to add insult to injury? Write something rude on a plaster cast.

McTavish: How was that Caribbean cruise ye won in that competition?
McGregor: Terrible. For the first three days I didnae eat a thing.
McTavish: Seasick?
McTavish: No, I didn't realise the meals were included free.

My wife said to me 'you'll drive me to my grave.' I had the car ready in two minutes.

My mother in law says she'll dance on my grave. It doesn't bother me, I'm getting buried at sea.

A man was squeezed into the narrow back seat of a small taxi, with his very fat wife.
'I bet you wish you'd married a slimmer woman!' she joked.
'I did,' he replied.

Cohen and Goldberg were crossing the English Channel in a ferry when a huge storm blew up. The boat was pitched and tossed about like a toy as the waves crashed over the decks. Cohen clutched Goldberg and said 'I'm terrified the ship's going to sink!' 'Why worry already?' said Goldberg. 'Is it your ship?'

People who work on make-up counters are so smug about their jobs. They're always rubbing it in customers' faces.

'My wife's one of twins.'
'How can you tell them apart?'
'Her brother's got a moustache.'

'My wife says I'm a chauvinist pig who thinks a woman's place is in the kitchen.'
'Why don't you buy her something to make her feel more appreciated. What's her favourite flower?'
'Self-raising, I think.'

A conjuror was performing on a cruise ship. After the first trick, a heckler shouted 'It's up your sleeve!' The conjuror was annoyed but carried on to his next trick. 'It's under the table!' yelled the heckler. This went on for several more tricks until suddenly, the ship's boiler exploded. Half an hour later the conjuror and the heckler were clinging to some wreckage in the sea. The heckler said 'Alright, I give up. What did you do with the ship?'

'My new car's got everything. Alloys, turbo charge, bucket seats, and GPS over-ride.'
'What on earth's a GPS over-ride?'
'My wife.'

A married couple were sitting on the sofa sipping wine. Out of the blue, the wife said 'I love you.'

'Is that you or the wine talking?' asked the husband.

'It's me,' replied the wife. 'Talking to the wine.'

'That's a nice new locket. Is there some sort of memento inside?

'A lock of my husband's hair.'

'But he's still alive!'

'Yes, but his hair is gone.'

Tramp (to businessman): Lend me a tenner until payday, guv?

Businessman: Hmm, when's payday?

Tramp: How should I know? You're the one with a job!

'If I were to die first,' said a woman to her husband, 'would you ever marry again?'

'Well...I suppose it's possible.' replied the man.

'And would you live in this house?'

'Can't see why not.'

'And would you sleep in our bed?'

'No point buying a new one.'

'I bet you'd even let her wear my clothes, wouldn't you?'

'No, she's smaller than you.'

A woman was in the kitchen frying some eggs when her husband came up beside her.

'Not too much gas, dear, turn it down a bit....flip the eggs over now, quickly, or they'll stick...move them round the pan more, or the edges will go all brown...watch out for that grease on the side of the pan! Turn off the gas now – turn it off! Turn it off! Hurry up or they'll be burnt!'

'What on earth is wrong with you?' said his wife.

'Nothing,' replied the husband calmly. 'I just wanted to show you what it feels like when I'm driving.'

A man was with his wife in a romantic restaurant.

'Darling, you look wonderful in this candlelight,' he said to her.

'Oh darling. That's such a sweet thing to say,' she replied.

'Yes,' said the man. 'We'll have to get some candles at home.'

'All my husband and I do is argue. I'm so worried about it, I've lost at least half a stone.'

'Why don't you just leave him?'

'I'd like to lose another half a stone first.'

'If I had a rabbit in a hutch, and I bought another rabbit, how many rabbits would I have?'

'Why, two, of course'

'No, ten.

'You don't know your arithmetic'

'You don't know my rabbits.'

A man went into a restaurant and said to the waiter, 'I'll have the tomato soup, the roast beef with gravy, and the apple crumble and custard.' 'Why sir,' replied the waiter, 'how do you know we serve all that? You haven't even looked at the menu.' 'No,' replied the man, 'but I've looked at the tablecloth.'

My wife went to the beauty parlour and got a mud pack. She looked great for three days – then the mud fell off.

A man who compromises when he's wrong is wise; a man who compromises when he's right is married.

Wife: I want a boob job.
Husband: What's wrong with the job you've got?

Smith: If it wasn't for that moustache you'd look just like my wife.
Jones: I haven't got a moustache.
Smith: No, but my wife has.

A religious young lady came home from a date, rather sad. She told her mother, 'John proposed to me an hour ago.'
'Then why are you so sad?' her mother asked.
'Because he also told me he was an atheist. Mother, he doesn't even believe there's a hell.'

Her mother replied, 'Marry him anyway. Between the two of us, we'll show him how wrong he is.'

Wife (to husband): We're not going to Spain on holiday again. The climate disagrees with mother.
Husband: That must be the bravest climate in the world!

A father left work a little late one night and, while on his way home, he remembered that he had not yet purchased a Christmas gift for his little daughter. He dashed into a toy shop and asked the assistant, 'How much is the Barbie doll in the window?'
The assistant replied, 'We have "Barbie goes to the gym" for £19.95, "Barbie plays Golf" for £19.95, "Barbie goes Shopping" for £19.95, "Barbie goes to the Beach" for £19.95, and "Divorced Barbie" for £299.99.'
The man was shocked and asked, 'Why does the divorced Barbie cost £299.99 when the rest are only £19.95?'
The assistant replied, 'Because "Divorced Barbie" comes with Ken's car, Ken's house, Ken's boat, Ken's furniture, Ken's computer, and one of Ken's friends.'

'I wish I'd listened to what my mother told me.'
'Why, what did she tell you?'
'I don't know. I didn't listen.'

In the old Highlands McTavish awoke early one morning to find his wife had died in the night. With admirable presence of mind, he called out to his servant: 'Maggy, you'll only need to cook the one egg for breakfast this morning.'

Two Scotsmen were walking through a rough part of Glasgow and saw a gang of youths approaching them.
'I think we're going tae get mugged here, Sandy,' said one.
'I think ye're right, Donald,' said the other, passing him a wad of cash. 'Here's that hundred poond I owe ye.'

Customer: (to chemist) I'd like a bar of soap please.
Chemist: Would you like it scented?
Customer: No, I'll take it with me now.

Recent research shows up to 25% of American women are receiving professional therapy for 'shopping addiction'. This is a terrifying statistic, as it shows that the other 75% are going untreated.

Smith: My father was very particular about my education. He wanted me to have all the opportunities he never had.
Jones: Did he send you to Eton?
Smith: No, to a girls' school.

Murphy went for a job on a building site. 'You'll need to be able to make tea and drive a four ton truck,' said the foreman.
'Jaysus,' said Murphy. 'How big is the teapot?!'

First vicar: I keep hearing on the TV adverts that this Christmas will be the greatest ever.
Second vicar: I rather thought that was the first one?

Seamus and Paddy had too much to drink and decided to spend the night at a hotel in Dublin. They asked for a room with two single beds. It was dark and they couldn't find the light switch in the room. They were so drunk they both got into the same bed without realising. A few seconds later Seamus said 'Paddy, wake up. There's someone in my bed wit me.'
There was a pause and Paddy said 'There's someone in my bed as well!'
'Tell you what Paddy,' said Seamus, 'you tip that feller out of your bed and I'll tip that feller out of my bed!'
So Paddy pushed Seamus out of bed onto the floor.
Seamus howled with pain and said 'Paddy, the one in my bed's only gone and tipped me out before I tipped him out!'
'Sure never mind,' said Paddy. 'You can get in with me!'

'Every night when I go to bed, I think about plumbing.'
'Do you think you'll pursue it as a career?'
'No, it's just a pipe dream.'

'How dare you drink before me!' said the judge to the drunk who had just swigged from a bottle in court. 'I'm sorry yeronnner,' replied the man, passing the bottle to the judge. 'I should have offered you a drink first!'

Quasimodo walked into a pub and ordered a whisky.
'Bell's all right?' asked the barman.
'Don't talk shop,' said Quasimodo.

A man walked into a pub and saw an impressive stuffed bull's head on the wall above the bar. The landlord saw the man looking at it and said 'That bull killed my father.' 'Was he a bull fighter?' asked the man.' No,' replied the landlord. 'He was standing there under it and it fell on him.'

'I know a man who eats nothing but Chinese food.'
'Why's that?'
'He's a Chinaman.'

A drunken husband was singing his wife's praises to the assembled dinner guests. 'My dear wife thinks of everything. Why, to make my life easier, she even installed a special light in the bathroom, which comes on automatically whenever I have to go in the middle of the night.'
The wife gasped with horror. 'So it's YOU that's been peeing in the fridge!'

A toilet has been stolen from a police station in Letchworth, Herts. Police say they have nothing to go on.

A woman was disturbed at breakfast by the bin men outside and realised she'd forgotten to leave her dustbin out on the pavement to be emptied.

She rushed out into the street in her old dressing gown stained with egg, a cigarette end dangling from her mouth and her hair full of curlers, and the remains of a mud mask on her face from the night before.

'Am I too late for the rubbish collection?' she asked.

'No love,' replied the binman. 'Jump in!'

A man walked into a barber's and asked to have his hair cut like David Beckham.

Twenty minutes later the man's hair was chopped unevenly with a ragged fringe and razor nicks around the ears. Disgusted, the man said 'This is awful – David Beckham's hair doesn't look like this!'

'It would if he had it cut in here,' said the barber.

On a beautiful summer's day, two English tourists were driving through Wales.

At Llanfairpwllgwyngyllgogerychwyrndrobwyllllantysiliogogogoch they stopped for lunch and one of the tourists asked the waitress: 'Before we order, I wonder if you could settle an argument for us. Can you pronounce where we are, very, very, very slowly?'

The girl leaned over and said:
'Burrr… gurrr… King.'

A man walked into a hairdresser's and said 'give me a Tony Curtis.'
The barber shaved all the man's hair off and left him totally bald. When the man looked in the mirror he recoiled in shock. 'Don't you know what Tony Curtis looks like?' he shouted.
'I should do,' said the barber. 'I saw 'The King and I' fourteen times!'

The barber tried to sell me a tortoiseshell comb. I can't imagine what it's for, all the tortoise shells I've seen have been bald.

They say contentment is wealth. But you can't spend it.

'How's your new job?'
'I've got 500 people under me.'
'Sounds important!'
'No, I'm cutting the grass at the cemetery'

A woman took an old photograph of her late mother to a photographer and asked if it could be enlarged. 'Certainly madam', said the photographer, 'come back next Wednesday and it will be ready.' 'There's just one thing' said the woman. 'I never liked that

hat she's got on in the picture. Could you take it out?' The photographer looked at the picture and said 'yes, I think we can do that by airbrushing. But I'll need to know what sort of hairstyle she had.' 'Well you'll see that when you take the hat out!' replied the customer.

A few years ago we had Steve Jobs, Bob Hope and Johnny Cash. Now we have no Jobs, no Hope and no Cash.

A retired couple consulted with an architect to build their dream home.
The wife pointed to the plans. 'This window here means that the neighbours will be able to see me in the shower!' she said in horror.
'Don't worry dear,' said her husband. 'They'll only look once.'

My wife gave me one of those badger shaving brushes for Christmas. I said what do I want to go shaving badgers for?

'Where are you going with your dog?'
'I'm taking him to the vets to have him put down.'
'Is he mad?'
'Well he's not very happy about it.'

A fool and his money are hard to find.

There was a beautiful young woman knocking on my hotel room door all night. I finally had to let her out.

Pupil: 'Who was that lady I seed you with last night?'
Teacher: '"I saw, I saw"'.
Pupil: 'Alright then, who was that eyesore I seed you with last night?'

An elderly lady was describing how she and her husband had met and fallen in love at the old people's home. 'We talked to each other and just clicked,' she said.
'Yes,' added the husband. 'Elbows, knees and hips.'

Wife: How come you never bring me flowers?
Husband: What's the point? They could be dead in a week.
Wife: So could you, but I still like having you around.

The Welsh Guards were surrounded by Zulus. The soldiers fought desperately as the spears flew thick and fast. Young Private Evans stood up and began singing 'Men of Harlech' and more spears flew at them, killing Evans.
Private Jones stood up and began to sing 'All Through the Night'. A spear cut him down instantly.
Private Davies stood up and before he could open his mouth the officer shouted 'For God's sake man sing them something they like!'

Three Welshmen were in a pub praising the beer.
Jones: Best glass of beer I never tasted no better.
Evans: So did I neither.
Davies: 'Neither did I too.

What did Quasimodo get when he retired?
A lump sum and forty years' back pay.

What's the best way to ensure a letter of complaint to Royal Mail gets looked at?
Put it inside a birthday card.

Definition of old: someone who still remembers when he knew more than his phone.

'Where were you born?'
'London.'
'What part?'
'All of me.'

On their silver wedding anniversary the wealthy heiress said to her husband, 'now look me in the eye and tell me honestly, that you didn't marry me for my money.' 'I didn't,' replied her husband, 'but by this time I think I've earned it.'

Two women friends met after many years.
'Tell me,' said one, 'What happened to your son?'
'My son? the poor, poor boy!' sighed the other. 'He unfortunately married a girl who won't do a thing around the house. She won't cook, she won't clean. All she does is lie on the sofa watching TV. The poor boy even has to bring her breakfast in bed, would you believe it?'
'That's really awful!'
'And what about your daughter?'
'Ah, now she's the lucky one! She married an angel. He won't let her do anything in the house. He does all the cooking and cleaning. And each morning he brings her breakfast in bed, would you believe it? Then all she has to do is spend the whole day with her feet up watching TV.'

I think my wife would divorce me, if she could find a way of doing it without making me happy.

A man walked into a bar on the top floor of the hotel he was staying in. He sat down next to a drunk who said; 'you see that window over there? If you jump out you fly back in.'
'Prove it,' the man said. So the drunk dived out the window and flew back in.
The man was amazed and immediately jumped out of the window, fell fifty stories to the pavement and was killed instantly.
The barman looked over and sighed.
'You're a real nuisance when you're drunk, Superman.'

'Where are you going on holiday this year?'
'Spain, in August.'
'Spain in August! You'll hate it. It'll be a hundred degrees in the shade.'
'Well I don't have to stay in the shade, do I?'

'I once knew a man with one leg called Levitsky.'
'What was his other leg called?'

You can tell a lot about a woman from her hands. For instance, if they're placed around your throat, she's probably quite annoyed.

'How was your blind date?'
'Terrible! He showed up in a 1932 Rolls-Royce.'
'What's so terrible about that?'
'He was the original owner.'

My hamster died yesterday. He fell asleep at the wheel.

A tramp knocked on the back door of a large house. The wealthy lady of the house answered the door. 'Yes?' she said imperiously, looking at the shabby visitor.
'Sorry to bother you missus, but I haven't eaten for three days. Could you spare a few pence?'

'I'm sorry,' replied the lady, 'but I don't give money to beggars. However, if you are willing to work, there are one or two jobs that need to be done around the place.'

'Right you are missus,' said the man. 'I'm willing to work fer me keep.'

'Good,' said the lady. She handed him some sandpaper, a tin of paint and a brush. 'Go round to the front of the house and repaint the porch.'

Off went the tramp. An hour later he returned with a big smile on his face and his hand held out. 'I've done the job like you said missus. But by the way, it's not a porch, it's a Ferrari.'

Welshman: I will now sing 'All through the night'.
Englishman: Couldn't you finish a bit earlier?

Enid met her old friend Deirdre at a school reunion.
'My dear,' said Deirdre, 'you haven't changed a bit in forty years!'
'Good Lord,' replied Enid. 'You mean I looked like this forty years ago?'

Stan feared his wife Mavis wasn't hearing as well as she used to and he thought she might need a hearing aid. Not quite sure how to approach her, he called the doctor to discuss the problem. The doctor told him there was a simple informal test the husband could perform before bothering with a full examination in the surgery.

'Here's what you do,' said the doctor. 'Stand about 20 feet away from her, and in a normal conversational speaking tone see if she hears you. If not, go to 10 feet, then 5 feet, and so on until you get a response.'

That evening, Mavis was in the kitchen cooking dinner and Stan was in the living room, about 20 feet away. He decided to try the test. 'What's for dinner, Mavis?' he said.

No response.

So he moved closer to the kitchen, and repeated 'Mavis, what's for dinner?' Still no response.

Next he moved right into the kitchen, just five feet behind his wife, and said 'Mavis, what's for dinner?'

Again he gets no response.

Finally he walked right up behind her. 'Mavis, what's for dinner?'
'FOR THE FOURTH TIME STAN, IT'S SHEPHERD'S PIE!'

Customer (in restaurant): Waiter, this chicken must be at least ten years old!
Waiter: How can you tell?
Customer: By the teeth.
Waiter: But chickens don't have teeth.
Customer: No, but I do!

During Sunday service the vicar stood up and said 'It is with great regret that I have to announce that our long standing treasurer, Mr Greenhill, has absconded with the organist's wife and half the church funds.' There was a gasp from the congregation as the clergyman continued. 'We will now sing hymn number 634, 'There is a green hill far away.'

Newsflash: a Lancashire woman is suing her local hospital after her husband underwent an operation which she claimed caused him to lose interest in sex. A hospital spokesman said all they had done was perform routine cataract surgery which had improved his eyesight.

A man and his nagging wife went to Honolulu on holiday. Soon they began to argue about the correct way to pronounce the word 'Hawaii.' The man insisted that it was pronounced Hawaii, with a 'w' sound. The wife said it was pronounced like 'Havaii,' with a 'v' sound. Finally, they saw an old native on the beach, and asked him which was correct. The old man said 'it's "Havaii."'
'You idiot,' the wife said to her husband. 'I told you I was right!' As they left she thanked the old man.
He replied 'you're velcome.'

An eighteenth-century vagabond, exhausted and famished, came to a roadside inn with a sign reading: 'George and the Dragon.' He knocked. The innkeeper's wife stuck her head out a window. 'Could ye spare some victuals?' He asked. The woman glanced at his shabby, dirty clothes. 'No!' she shouted. 'Could I have a pint of ale?' 'No!' she shouted. 'Could I at least sleep in your stable?' 'No!' she shouted again. The vagabond said, 'Might I please...?' 'What now?' the woman screeched, not allowing him to finish. 'D'ye suppose,' he asked, 'that I might have a word with George?'

Evans was watching a rugby game in Cardiff.

In the packed stadium there was only one empty seat, right next to him.

'Whose is that seat?' asked a man in the row behind.

'I got the ticket for my wife,' said Evans. 'But she died in an accident.'

'So you're keeping the seat vacant as a mark of respect?'

'No,' said the fan, 'I offered it to all of my friends.'

'So why didn't they take it?'

'They've all gone to the funeral.'

My wife asked me if I was having an affair with a woman from Llanfairpwllgwyngyllgogerychwyrndrobwyllllatysiliogogogoch.

I said: 'How can you say such a thing?'

The great dramatist J.B. Priestley is said to have attended a performance of one of his plays, but for reasons unknown decided to leave the theatre before the show ended. On hearing this, the lead actor exclaimed 'if that's the way he feels about the play, he shouldn't have written it!'

A man and his wife stayed on a farm one summer. They enjoyed it but were doubtful about going back there the following year because of the smell of the pig-sty next to the house.

The man wrote to the farmer about it and the farmer replied:

'We haven't had any pigs on the farm since you were here last summer. Do come again.'

Drunk (to barman): Can you recommend a good port?
Barman: Yes – Southampton – there's a train leaving in ten minutes!

A businessman was staying in a small Alpine town for a few days. One night he felt a bit lonely and asked the pub landlord if there were any loose women he could visit.

'They've all been driven out by the new priest,' said the man sadly. 'But one or two are still working in the old cave on the edge of town. All you do is go into the cave and whistle. If you hear a whistle coming back, you're in luck.'

The businessman eagerly went on his way. It was a dark night and he had trouble finding the cave but eventually he got inside and whistled. He was delighted to hear a whistle come back. Two seconds later he was knocked down by an express train.

I once had a Welsh girlfriend with 36DDs. It was the longest surname I've ever seen.

A Scotsman and an Englishman met in London, both penniless, both thirsty.

The Englishman had an idea for getting a free drink: 'I know a barmaid in a pub near here who has got a very bad memory. If you get her involved in a conversation she can't remember whether you've paid or not. Let me try it on first.'

The Englishman went into the pub and duly got his free drink. Then it was the Scotsman's turn to try.

He went over to the bar, ordered his pint and began to tell the barmaid all about life in the Highlands. Ten minutes later he drained his glass and said to the barmaid:
'Well, it's been nice talking to you but I've got to be off now. What about my change?'

Sergeant (to new army recruit): What would you do if somebody attacked you with a rifle butt?
Recruit: But what?

'My husband's just died, worth a million pounds.'
'Sorry to hear that. Did he leave you much?'
'Oh, about twice a month.'

A man went into a garage and said to the mechanic, 'I need a new 710 cap for my car engine, the old one's broken,'
The mechanic scratched his head. 'I've never heard of one of those. What make is it?'
'A BMW 5 series,' replied the man.
'What's the thing called again?'
'A 710 cap,' replied the man, getting a little impatient. 'Look, I've got it in my pocket.'
He handed a small disk to the mechanic who looked at it for a moment then turned the disk round.
'You've been reading it upside down. That's an OIL cap!'

A Scotsman went into a butcher's and asked for ten pence worth of steak.

Surprised at the small amount, the butcher asked 'ten pence worth of steak? What do you want it for?'

'Five pence.'

A story is told of Sir Noel Coward's reaction after he received some bad press. He wrote to the critic 'I have just read your upsetting review in the smallest room in the house, but I managed to put it all behind me.'

An old man walked into a shoe mender's and said 'In 1939 my father left a pair of shoes here but then he went off to the war and was killed. Have you still got them?' Thinking it must be a joke, the cobbler laughed. 'Have you got a ticket?'

The man solemnly produced a faded ticket from his wallet and placed it on the counter. 'We found this amongst my mother's things when she died some weeks ago. She'd kept it all these years.'

The cobbler realised the man was serious. He examined the ticket and scratched his head.

'Look sir, this place has changed hands dozens of times since 1939,' he said, 'but I'll see if I can find them.'

He went down to the cellar and rummaged around in the far corners until he finally found the shoes in a cupboard. He emerged from the cellar waving them triumphantly.

'I've found them,' he cried, as he blew the dust off them. 'Ready next Thursday.'

On one occasion, a man making heavy breathing sounds from a phone box told the worried operator: 'I haven't got a pen so I'm steaming up the window to write the number on.'

Marriage isn't a word, it's a sentence.

Give a man a fish and he will eat for a day. Teach him how to fish, and he will sit by a canal and drink beer all day.

First farmer: Do you find it pays to keep a cow?
Second farmer: Oh yes. Mine makes two gallons of milk a day.
First farmer: And how much of that do you sell?
Second farmer: Four gallons.

Two Yorkshiremen were talking in the pub. 'There's a terrible smell in our house,' said Stan.
'Why's that?' said Bert.
'Well,' replied Stan, 'it's the fault of the missus. She keeps her six cats int' front room and they stink t'place out.'
'Canst thou not open t'window in't room?' replied Bert.
'Nay!' said Stan. 'Don't be daft. Then all me pigeons would fly out!'

Doctor: I haven't seen you for a long time.
Patient: I know, I've been ill.

Customer (in pet shop): I want a thousand cockroaches.
Shopkeeper: What on earth do you want them for?
Customer: My tenancy expires today and the contract says I have to leave the house exactly as I found it.

Paddy and Seamus were up from County Kerry on the spree in Dublin and were the worse for wear. They got into a taxi, demanding to be taken to Temple Bar. They slumped forward in their seats, semi-conscious.

The driver didn't want two drunks in his cab and guessed they were too sozzled to know where they were, so instead of moving the vehicle he just revved the engine loudly a few times then switched it off and shouted 'here we are fellers.'

'Thanks a million, that was nice and quick!' said Paddy, and staggered out of the cab, none the wiser. But Paddy stopped, leant through the partition and grabbed the driver by the scruff of his neck.

'What the hell do you tink you're playing at!' he slurred. The taxi driver thought for a moment he'd been rumbled until Paddy continued. 'You drove so fast you could have killed us!'

Woman (to gym instructor): Can you teach me to do the splits?
Gym instructor: How flexible are you?
Woman: I can't do Wednesdays or Fridays.

The definition of 'mixed feelings': seeing your mother in law drive your brand new car over a cliff.

A man walks into a bar with a roll of tarmac under his arm and says: 'Pint please, and one for the road.'

When the inventor of the drawing board messed things up, what did he go back to?

I cleaned the attic with the wife the other day. Now I can't get the cobwebs out of her hair.

Barber (to customer): That'll be ten pounds, sir.
Customer: Ten pounds? Look here, the sign in your window says "High class hair cut, five pounds."'
Barber: I know, but your hair's not high class.

A university teacher wrote these words on the blackboard: 'woman without her man is nothing'. The teacher then asked the students to punctuate the words correctly.
The men wrote: 'Woman, without her man, is nothing.'
The women wrote: 'Woman! Without her, man is nothing.'

While he was visiting his son, an old man asked for the password to the wi-fi.
'It's taped under the keyboard,' said his son.
After three failed attempts to log on, the man asked, 'Am I spelling this right? T-A-P-E-D-U-N-D-E-R-T-H-E-K-E-Y-B-O-A-R-D?

What did they call the boy who finally stood up to the school bully?

An ambulance.

The phone was ringing so I picked it up and said 'Who's speaking please?' and the caller said 'you are.'

A policeman asked two drunks for their names and addresses. The first answered, 'I'm Paddy O'Riley, of no fixed abode.' The second replied, 'I'm Seamus O'Toole, and I live in the flat above Paddy.'

One dark night a teenager took a shortcut home through the cemetery. Halfway across, he was startled by a tapping noise coming from the misty shadows. Trembling with fear, he saw an old man with a hammer and chisel, chipping away at a head-stone.

'I thought you were a ghost,' said the relieved teen. 'What are you doing working so late?'

'Oh, those idiots,' grumbled the old man. 'They misspelt my name!'

A professor was trying to instruct the class in the very important duty of cultivating the faculty of observation. To emphasize his point he mixed a very noxious compound in a basin and then said, 'I want you to all observe what I do and then come forward and do exactly the same thing.'

He dipped his finger into the basin and put it into his mouth, making a very wry face. Each member of the class came to his desk and dipped a finger into the bowl, placed it in the mouth and departed for his seat with a very disgusted expression of countenance.

When all were seated once more the professor said, 'None of you observed what I did, for, had you done so, you would have perceived that the finger I put in my mouth was not the one I dipped into the basin.'

A girl was crying bitterly.
Mother: What happened dear?
Daughter: Mummy do I look like a wicked witch?
Mother: No!
Daughter: Are my eyes all funny?
Mother: No!
Daughter: Is my nose big?
Mother: No dearest!
Daughter: Am I fat?
Mother: You are a beautiful little girl!
Daughter: Then why do people keep telling me I look so much like you?

Husband: I've just seen our daughter knitting baby clothes.
Wife: Thank heavens for that. She's finally started doing something other than chase men around.

Farmer Giles was complaining to a friend about his new bull.'All that bull does is eat grass. Won't even look at a cow.'

'Take him to the vet,' his friend suggested.

The next week, Farmer Giles was much happier. 'The vet gave him some pills, and the bull serviced all of my cows!' he told his friend. 'Then he broke through the fence and bred with all my neighbour's cows!'

'What kind of pills were they?' asked the friend.

'I don't know,' said the farmer,' but they've got a minty taste.'

Doctor: Do you want the good news or the bad news first?

Patient: Give me the good news.

Doctor: You're going to have a disease named after you.

When my wife gets a little upset, sometimes a simple 'Calm down' in a soothing voice is all it takes to get her a lot upset.

Two days before her birthday, a wife said to her husband meaningfully, 'last night I dreamt I received a diamond necklace. What do you suppose that means?'

The husband thought for a moment then said with a smile, 'perhaps you'll find out on your birthday.'

With mounting excitement, the wife opened a package from her husband on her birthday.

Inside was a book entitled 'How to Interpret Dreams.'

'My wife is on a three week diet.'
'How much has she lost so far?'
'Two weeks.'

'I lost my dog last night. What should I do?'
'Put a poster on a tree.'
'Why? He can't read.'

Paddy was at a Dublin specialist for an examination. The nurse handed him a small plastic bottle and told him to urinate in it.
'Sure and not in front of all these people?' said Paddy in a shocked voice.
'Certainly not,' replied the nurse, pointing to the lavatory. 'Do it in that room.'
A few minutes later Paddy emerged and handed the nurse the empty bottle.
'Turns out I didn't need it,' he said. 'There was a toilet in there.'

A politician was on a tour of a psychiatric hospital. He asked the director how they decided if a patient needed to be committed.
'Well,' the director said, 'we fill a bath with water, then offer the patient a teaspoon, a teacup and a bucket, and ask him to empty the tub.'
'I see,' the politician said. 'A normal person would use the bucket because it's the biggest.'
'No,' the director said. 'A normal person would pull the plug.'

Doctor (to receptionist): Have you seen my auroscope?
Receptionist: No! Does it say anything good?

McTavish set up his stall at the car boot sale. After a while he had to answer the call of nature, so asked his friend McDougal at the next stall to mind his things for him.
'Whatever ye do, if someone wants those bagpipes, make sure you get a good price for them.'
'Alright, but if someone wants to haggle, how low are ye willing to go?' asked McDougal.
'Weelll...try for £50, but I'm willing to accept £20.'
A few minutes later McTavish returned and was surprised to see the bagpipes were gone.
'How much did ye get for the bagpipes?' asked McTavish.
'Twenty poond,' replied McDougal.
'Who bought them?'
'I did.'

Smith: Why do you call your car 'Daisy'?
Jones: Well, some days 'e starts, and some days 'e doesn't!

Sunday school teacher: Can anyone tell me what an evangelist is?
Little Johnny: Someone who plays the evangelo.

Bert and Mavis were getting married at the grand old ages of 95 and 94 respectively.

Before the wedding, they visited the local chemist.

'Do you sell heart medication?' asked Bert.

'Of course,' replied the chemist.

'What about pills for arthritis and lumbago?' asked Mavis.

'Certainly,' the chemist said.

'How about corn plasters, surgical stockings and back rests?' enquired Bert.

'Yes, we've got all those,' the chemist said.

'Do you have wheelchairs and zimmer frames?' asked Mavis.

'We've got plenty of those in the back room,' replied the chemist.

'That's great,' said Bert. 'There's just one more question.'

'What's that?' asked the chemist, wondering what on earth more they could require.

'Can we have our wedding list here?'

Who earns a living by driving his customers away?
A taxi driver.

A military man had been posted overseas for five years. He got an early discharge and came back to England, looking forward to seeing his wife and daughter who'd only been a baby when he left. He phoned ahead to tell his wife he'd be arriving home sooner than expected.

'Hello?' said a little girl's voice.

'Hello, it's your Daddy,' said the man. 'Is mummy near the phone?'

'No, Daddy. She's upstairs in the bedroom with Uncle Geoff.'
After a brief pause, the man said, 'But you don't have an Uncle Geoff!'
'Yes I do. He's upstairs in the bedroom with Mummy!'
The man thought quickly. ' Here's what I want you to do. Put down the phone, run upstairs, knock on the bedroom door and shout in to Mummy and Uncle Geoff that a man has just opened the front door and he says he's your daddy.'
'Okay, Daddy!'
A few minutes later, the little girl came back to the phone. 'Well, I did what you said, Daddy.'
'And what happened?'
'Well, Mummy jumped out of bed with no clothes on and ran around screaming, then she tripped over the rug and went out the back window and now she's all dead.'
'Oh my god! What about Uncle Geoff?'
'He jumped out of bed with no clothes on too and he was all scared and he jumped out the back window into the river, and now he's dead too.'
There was a long pause, then the man said, 'River? Is this Aylesbury 31227?'

Customer (in chemist's shop): Have you got anything to cure worms?
Chemist: I don't know – what's wrong with them exactly?

What is heavy forwards but not backwards?
Ton

A drunk was eating alone at a restaurant. He ordered the most expensive meal on the menu and called out 'drinks on the house for everybody!' His fellow diners were delighted. Half an hour later he ordered another bottle of champagne for himself and said 'drinks on the house for everybody!' again.

He ran up a huge bill and when it was time to pay, he simply smiled at the waiter and said 'I've got no money!' The waiter was furious and dragged the man into the kitchen, punched him in the face and smashed a frying pan over his head, then pulled him out through the restaurant to the front door. Before he could throw him out the man shouted to the other diners again 'Drinks on the house for everybody!'

Then he turned to the waiter and said 'But not for you – when you drink you get nasty!'

Did you hear about the calendar printer? He got fired for taking a day off.

I phoned the local builders today, I said to them 'Can I have a skip outside my house?' He said, 'I'm not stopping you!'

First vicar: What's the difference between a terrorist and an organist?
Second vicar: You can negotiate with a terrorist.

Change is inevitable, except from a vending machine.

Judge (to defendant): You stand accused of shooting your mother-in-law while drunk. Can't you see the terrible effect alcohol has had on you?
Defendant: I'll say. It made me miss!

Did you hear about the hungry clock? It went back four seconds.

A man walked into a bar and asked for an orange juice.
'Still orange?' said the barman?
'Well I haven't just changed my mind,' replied the man.

Paddy went to London and got talking to a man in a pub. The man said 'I'll bet you a fiver you can't solve this riddle. I'm looking at a portrait of a man and I say 'Brothers and sisters have I none, but that man's father is my father's son.' Who's the man in the picture?'
Paddy thought for a long while. 'Ah bejaysus,' he said 'sure and that's a difficult one. Here's the five pounds, I give up, what's the answer?'
'I'm looking at a picture of myself,' replied the man.
Paddy was impressed and decided he'd try this one out when he got home. So back in Dublin he met his old pal Seamus and said 'You'll never solve this one. I'm looking at a portrait of a man and I says to meself, 'Brothers and sisters have I none, but that man's father is my father's son.' Who's the man in the picture?'
'Sure and that's easy, I've heard this one before!' said Seamus. 'It's you!'

'That's where you're wrong!' cried Paddy. 'It's a feller I met in a pub in London!'

Hiker (to girl struggling to lead a cow): Where are you going with that cow?
Girl: Taking her to the bull.
Hiker: Can't the farmer do that?
Girl: Oh no, it has to be the bull.

Patient: I'm very worried about my brother, doctor. He thinks he's an orange.
Psychiatrist: Well you'd better fetch him here and I'll examine him.
Patient: There's no need, doctor. I've got him here in my pocket!

When the gorilla died in the zoo, the zookeeper hired a student to put on an ape costume and act like a gorilla until he could find a new one.
In his cage, the student pranced about, made noises and generally threw himself into the part, drawing a big crowd. He then climbed onto the fence of the neighbouring lion's cage, infuriating the animal. Suddenly he lost his footing and fell into the lion's den.
Terrified, the student shouted for help. The lion pounced, opened its jaws and whispered, 'Shut up! Do you want to get us both fired?!'

A husband and wife had been married for 50 years. The woman kept in the wardrobe a shoe box that she forbade her husband from ever opening. But when she was on her deathbed she asked him to open the box.

Inside was a knitted tea cosy and £20,000 in cash.

'My mother told me that the secret to a happy marriage was to never argue,' she explained. 'Instead, I should keep quiet and knit a tea cosy.'

Her husband was touched. Only one tea cosy was in the box— that meant she'd been angry with him only once in 50 years. 'But what about all this money?' he asked.

'Oh,' she said, 'that's the money I made from selling the tea cosies.'

Wife: You loved me before we were married.
Husband: Well, now it's your turn!

'I once knew an eccentric artist who painted a cobweb on the wall. It was so realistic that the cleaning lady spent three hours trying to clean it off.'
'Sorry, I don't believe it.'
'Well, artists are like that sometimes.'
'Yes, but cleaning ladies aren't.'

Coroner: What were your husband's last words?
Widow: 'I don't see how they can make a profit on vodka that costs 99p a bottle.'

Baby flower: Mummy, how did I get made?
Mummy flower: Why, the stalk brought you!

Customer(in chemist's shop): I'd like some talcum powder please.
Assistant: Certainly sir. Walk this way please.
Customer: If I could walk that way I wouldn't need the talcum powder!

'I'm going to the doctors, I don't like the look of my wife.'
'I'll come with you, I hate the sight of mine.'

Jones: I went out with a blonde the other day and she made me dizzy.
Smith: How's that?
Jones: Before I knew it I'd lost my bank balance.

'I don't know her to speak to, only to speak about.'

Definition of junk: something you keep for ten years and then throw away two weeks before you need it.

There are some people so addicted to exaggeration that they can't even tell the truth without lying.

'How was the bridge party last night?'
'It was fine until the police came and looked under the bridge!'

'The ball glanced off my head into the wicketkeeper's hands,' said the batsman on returning to the pavilion, 'and that fool of an umpire gave me out.' 'Well,' observed a teammate, 'sometimes they go by sound.'

Sign on spiritualist medium's front door: 'Please ring bell, as knocking can cause confusion.'

'Are your relatives in business?'
~Yes, in the iron and steel business'
'Oh, indeed?'
'Yes, me mother irons and me father steals'

A drunk phoned the police to report that thieves had been in his car. 'They've stolen the dashboard, the steering wheel, the brake pedal, even the accelerator,' he cried. 'Oh hang on,' he added. 'I'm in the back seat.'

A man went into a public convenience and sat down in one of the cubicles.
A voice from the next cubicle said 'Hi, how are you?'.
Embarrassed, the man said, 'I'm fine, thank you'.

The voice said 'So what are you up to?'

The man replied, 'Just doing the same as you - sitting here!'

The voice said 'Can I come over?'

By this time the man was annoyed and said 'I'm rather busy right now'.

Then the voice said, 'Listen, there's some idiot in the next cubicle answering all my questions. I'll have to call you back'.

Tourist (to pub landlord): When does the Loch Ness monster appear?

Landlord: Usually after six, sir.

Tourist: Six am or six pm?

Landlord: Six whiskies, sir.

I took my wife out for tea and biscuits the other day. It was alright but she didn't like the bit where she had to give blood.

Passenger: Is this the Barking bus?

Driver: No, it just goes 'toot toot!'

Paddy saw a piece of paper sticking to the top of a pillar box but it was too high to read, so he clambered up to the top. When he got to the paper, he saw that it said 'Wet Paint'.

Surgeon (to patient): Why are you so nervous?

Patient: Well doctor, it's my first operation.
Surgeon: Really? It's mine as well, but I feel fine.

Husband: Why can't you spend less on clothes? Just buy one good outfit and you'll save money.
Wife: That's just what I've been doing. I buy one good outfit every week.

A store that sells new husbands has opened in New York City , where a woman may go to choose a husband.
The entrance has a description of how the store operates:
You may visit this store ONLY ONCE! There are six floors and the value of the products increase as the shopper ascends the flights. The shopper may choose any item from a particular floor, or may choose to go up to the next floor, but you cannot go back down except to exit the building!
So, a woman went to the Husband Store to find a husband. On the first floor the sign on the door read:
Floor 1 – These men have jobs
She was intrigued, but continued to the second floor, where the sign read:
Floor 2 – These men have jobs and love kids.
'That's nice,' she thought , 'but I want more.' So she continued upwards.
The third floor sign read:
Floor 3 – These men have jobs, love kids, and are extremely good looking.
'Wow,' she thought, but kept going. She went to the fourth floor

and the sign read:

Floor 4 – These men have jobs, love kids, are drop-dead good looking and help with housework.

'Oh, mercy me!' she exclaimed, 'I can hardly stand it!' Still, she went to the fifth floor and the sign read:

Floor 5 – These men have jobs, love kids, are drop-dead gorgeous, help with housework, and have a strong romantic streak. Shewas tempted to stay, but she went to the sixth floor, where the sign read:

Floor 6 – You are visitor 31,456,012 to this floor. There are no men on this floor. This floor exists solely as proof that women are impossible to please. Thank you for shopping at the Husband Store.

Police constable: Madam, I must ask you to accompany me to the station.

Woman: Why, what have I done?

Police constable: Nothing, I'm just a bit scared of the dark.

'I made a small fortune betting on the horses today.'

'So why do you look so unhappy?'

'Because I started with a large fortune.'

A policeman stopped a drunk woman in the street. 'You're staggering,' he said. The woman looked him up and down. 'You're not so bad yourself, dear,' she replied.

Son (to father): Dad, are all married people unhappy?
Father: No son. Just the men.

I went to see my lawyer but he said he was very busy finishing a big case. Turned out there were only two bottles left.

The postman arrived at a little pub in Scotland and said to the landlord, 'Aye, but it's an awfy long hot walk up the hill here, and mighty thirsty work.' Taking the hint, the landlord poured him a glass of whisky. 'Where's the letters then?' asked the landlord. 'Oh there's no letters,' replied the postman, sipping the whisky, 'but it's still an awfy long hot walk up the hill.'

Editor (to new journalist): You should write so that the most ignorant person can understand what you mean.
Journalist: Well, what part of my copy don't you understand?

A man was talking to his girlfriend about his firm's cricket team. 'Jones is coming along nicely. In a few weeks he'll be our best man.'
'Oh darling,' said his girlfriend. 'What a lovely way to ask me.'

Husband: Come along dear, we'll be late for our appointment.
Wife: Don't be so impatient! I've been telling you for the last hour I'll only be five minutes.

A railway worker pocketed a tip from a passenger after helping him with his suitcase. The passenger said 'Do you know who I am?' 'No sir,' replied the porter. 'I'm the general manager of this railway,' continued the man. 'Don't you know it's clearly stated in the rule book that you can't take tips from passengers?' 'Yes sir,' replied the quick-thinking porter. 'But there's nothing that says I can't take a present from a colleague.'

McTavish looked depressed, so his friend McGregor asked what the trouble was. 'Mon,' said McTavish, 'I just walked ten miles to see the Cup Final.' 'Wheesht man,' replied McGregor. 'Think of the money ye saved on bus fares!' 'Aye, I know,' said McTavish. 'But by the time I got tae the stadium, I was too tired tae climb over the fence.'

Animal rights activist (to small boy): is that your mother over there in that fur coat?
Boy: Yes.
Activist: Don't you know a poor creature had to suffer to provide that coat?
Boy: Yes. It was Daddy.

McDougal was describing to McTavish how he'd been rescued from drowning in the loch. 'And then, just before they pulled me oot, ma whole life flashed before ma eyes, like a long line o' pictures!' 'Is that so?' replied McTavish. 'Ye didnae happen tae see a picture o' me lending ye a five pound note in 1957, did ye?'

My father gave most of his money to sick animals. The trouble was, he didn't know they were sick when he betted on them.

'Is your wife outspoken?'
'Not by anyone I know.'

'It's our fortieth wedding anniversary next week my dear,' said a man to his wife. 'What would you like as a present? A diamond necklace, a car, a world cruise?'
'I want a divorce,' said his wife.
'I wasn't planning on spending that much,' replied the man.

Scoutmaster: What's the best way to start a fire with two sticks?
Scout: Make sure one of them is a match.

My girlfriend dumped me because she didn't like my records. To this day I've still no idea how she got them from my doctor and probation officer.

An elderly couple had dinner at another couple's house, and after eating, the wives left the table and went into the kitchen. The two elderly gentlemen were talking, and one said, 'Last night we went out to a new restaurant, and it was really great. I would recommend it very highly.'
The other man said, 'What's the name of the restaurant?' The

first man thought hard, and finally said to his companion, 'What's the name of that red flower you give to someone you love?' His friend replied, 'A carnation?' 'No. No. The other one,' the man said. The other man offered another suggestion, 'A geranium?' 'No, said the man. 'You know the one that's red and has thorns.' His friend said, 'Do you mean a rose?' 'Yes, yes that's it. Thank you!' the first man said. He then turned towards the kitchen and yelled, 'Rose, what's the name of that restaurant we went to last night?'

'I took my wife on holiday to Bulgaria.'
'Sofia?'
'No, Maureen.'

'Is she a natural blonde or a platinum blonde?'
'Neither. She's a suicide blonde.'
'A suicide blonde? What's that?'
'Dyed by her own hand.'

Two students were talking. 'My father's offered to give me £5000 if I give up all my bad habits,' said one. 'Why do you look so un-happy then?' said his friend. 'Well,' said the other, 'if I give up all my bad habits, what am I going to spend £5000 on?'

Letter to agony aunt: 'I am a seventeen year old girl. Last night I stayed out very late with a boy and my mother was angry when

I got home. Did I do wrong?'
Reply: 'Try to remember!'

'Is that a popular song he's singing?'
'It was before he sang it.'

'My wife is the most wonderful woman in the world – and that's not just my opinion, it's hers as well!'

'I came home drunk last night and my wife had changed the locks.'
'That's terrible.'
'It gets worse. She'd changed the street we live on as well!'

Complaint to railway company: 'I was disgusted to find that the so-called "quiet carriage" on your trains makes the same annoying "diddly dum, diddly dee" noise as all the rest of them.'

They say prostitution is the world's oldest profession. If that's true, how did the men earn the money to pay for it?

'Spare some change, guv?'
'Sorry, I don't have any.'
'Aw go on. Just a few pence.'

'Really, I haven't any.'
'What do you want me to do? Beg for it?'

Paddy was getting married and realised he didn't have much experience with women. He went to a bookshop and bought a book entitled 'How to Hug.' Only three weeks later did he realise it was Volume 7 of the *Encyclopaedia Britannica.*

Doctor: (to elderly patient) How's your sex life?
Patient: Not bad. I have sex almost every day.
Doctor: Really?
Patient: Yes. Almost on Monday...almost on Tuesday...almost on Wednesday...

I love my wife terribly. Well, that's what she tells me anyway.

The teacher was explaining about vowels and consonants. 'Can anyone remember what the two kinds of letter in the alphabet are called?' Little Johnny put up his hand. 'Big ones and small ones.'

'I told my wife not to spend so much, but I got a sob story.'
'You mean she cried?'
'No, she just called me an S.O.B.'

The train was about to leave and the guard blew his whistle. 'Wait a minute!' called a young feminine voice. 'I'm still trying to get my clothes off!' All male eyes turned to the door, only to see a woman struggling to lift a large laundry bag onto the platform.

Daughter: Mother, what kind of husband should I look for?
Mother: You leave the husbands alone, and look for a single man!

Have you ever felt like going into an antique shop and saying 'what's new?'

Man proposes, but divorce exposes.

'Where have you been?'
'To the cemetery'.
'Good Lord – is somebody dead?'
'Yes, all of them.'

'I don't mind having my mother in law live with us. But I do wish she'd wait until we get married!'

An Englishman was on a walking holiday in Spain. He arrived at a small cafe in the country where he ordered tea. The tea arrived without milk. 'I can't possibly drink tea without milk,' thought the man; but he spoke no Spanish and the waiter spoke no English. After trying to make the waiter understand what he wanted without success, inspiration struck the man and he drew a picture of a cow on a paper napkin. The waiter smiled, nodded, and left the cafe. Twenty minutes later he came back with a ticket for a bullfight.

Paddy and Seamus were running a race to a tree, by different routes. 'If I get there first,' said Paddy, 'I'll make a mark on the tree with this chalk. If you get there first, you rub it off.'

Passenger on cruise ship (to steward): Is my wife forward?
Steward: Not with me, sir.

'My father made his fortune with his pen.'
'Oh really? Poetry or prose?'
'Neither – he was a pig farmer.'

He: You girls look much shorter in those bikinis.
She: Yes, and you men look much longer!

Admiral (to sailor): Are you a family man?
Sailor: Yes sir, I've got a wife and six children.
Admiral: Really. Don't you ever get homesick?
Sailor: Only when I'm at home, sir.

'Well I'll be damned,' said the river as the fat lady fell off the bridge.

An aspiring novelist sent a manuscript to a publisher with a note which read 'The characters in this story are purely fictional and bear no resemblance to anyone, living or dead.' A few days later the manuscript was returned. The editor had written on the note: 'That's what's wrong with it.'

They say 'ignorance of the law is no defence.' Unless you're a lawyer.

'She told me that you told her what I told you not to tell her.'
'I told her not to tell you I told her.'
'Oh dear. Well, don't tell her I told you that she told me.'

A hypochondriac told his doctor that he had a serious disease. 'Nonsense,' said the doctor. 'You wouldn't know if you had that – there are no symptoms until it's too late.' The patient replied, 'I know – that's why I'm worried I might have it.'

McTavish dreamt one night that he'd lent a man a hundred pounds. The next night, he was too afraid to go to sleep in case he dreamt he hadn't been paid back.

Seamus: I bet ye can't eat five pounds o'potatoes in one sittin'.
Paddy: Sure and I can. But only if they're small ones!

Prison chaplain (to convict): My good man, I hope you have realised the error of your ways.
Convict: I certainly have, padre. Next time, I'll wear gloves!

'We must learn to be satisfied with what we have,' said the vicar to one of his poor parishioners. 'Oh I am vicar,' said the man, 'it's what I haven't got that I'm dissatisfied with.'

Small boy (to father): Here's my report card. And just for reference, here's one of yours I found in the attic.

Curate (to vicar): Does your wife embroider church kneelers?
Vicar: No, but I'm told she adorned numerous pillows before I met her.

She: Did you ask my father for my hand in marriage?
He: Yes, I did it on the telephone.
She: What did he say?
He: 'I don't know who you are, but it's alright.'

A woman invested some money in a company which went bust.

With great shame she told her husband of the loss of £500. 'My dear,' said the man sadly, 'didn't I tell you always to consult me about whether to make an investment?'

'You did,' replied his wife.

'So why didn't you ask me?'

'I was worried you'd tell me not to.'

Judge (to defendant): Do you plead guilty or not guilty?

Defendant: I thought that's what you lot were supposed to find out!

A woman answered a knock at the door. 'Yes?' she said to the stranger standing there. 'Piano tuner, ma'am,' replied the man. 'But I didn't ask you to come,' said the woman. 'Besides, I can't afford to pay.' 'No problem ma'am,' said the man. 'The neighbours sent me and they paid in advance.'

Husband: Why don't we go south for the winter?

Wife: What for? We've got all the winter we need right here!

A tramp knocked on the door of a country cottage and asked for food. 'Come around to the back door,' said the lady of the house. The 'gentleman of the road' did so, but as he was about to enter the back garden, he noticed a bulldog in the corner. 'Will the dog bite?' said the tramp warily. 'I don't know,' said the woman. 'I've just bought him this morning and I'd like to find out.'

'My sister's just become a duchess.'
'Really – did she marry a duke?'
'No, a Dutchman.'

Woman (in photographer's studio): I wish to complain about the wedding photos you took. My husband looks like an ape!
Photographer: Well you should have thought of that before you married him!

'Did the doctor really mean it when he said you wouldn't live a week if you didn't stop chasing women?'
'He certainly did – I've been chasing his wife!'

Wife (to husband): Can you buy me a mousetrap?
Husband: I bought you one yesterday.
Wife: Yes, but that one's got a mouse in it.

'I see Jane's burning the candle at both ends again.'
'How?'
'Last week it was her birthday and she had 21 candles on the cake.'

'How do you know that he married her for her money?'
'I've seen her!'

'Why are you so late coming home?' said a woman to her drunken husband at midnight. 'Well my dear, you told me to walk straight back from the pub,' replied the man. 'I did,' said his wife angrily, 'but the pub closes at eleven. What have you been doing since then?' 'Waiting until I could walk straight,' replied the man.

Two elderly men were discussing their wives. 'My wife's gone, but not forgotten,' said one. The other sighed. 'My wife hasn't gone...and she hasn't forgotten either.'

They say a woman's work is never done. They're lucky. If a man's work was never done, he'd get the sack.

'My husband's no good at fixing things. So everything in our house works.'

'My wife's worried about having thirteen people to dinner tonight.'
'Superstitious, eh?'
'No, we've only got twelve matching plates.'

Corduroy pillows: They're making headlines!

'I remember the days when we all left our back doors unlocked,' recalled the elderly man. 'We weren't more honest; it's just that whenever anyone stole anything, we could always get it back, as the thieves always left their back doors open as well.'

Angry father: When I die, I shall leave you without a penny.
Son: Quite right. You can't take it with you!

Waiter: Dogs are not allowed in this restaurant, sir.
Man: That's not my dog.
Waiter: But he's following you.
Man: Well, so are you!

Man (on phone to doctor) Come quickly – my wife's about to have a baby!
Doctor: I'll come right away. Fetch lots of towels and boiling water.
Man: Why?
Doctor: Because it's raining outside and I'd like a cup of tea when I arrive.

The chief of a tribe of cannibals was asked why he had given up eating people. 'The British kept sending missionaries,' he explained, 'and you can't keep a good man down.'

Medium: The spirit of your wife wishes to speak with you.
Widower: You're a fake! My wife would never ask permission to

speak with me!

'Would you like to buy a raffle ticket sir? First prize is a week's holiday in Margate.'
'What's the second prize?'
'Two weeks' holiday in Margate.'

In the Great War an Irish regiment were marching through Belgium. Private O'Riley, half dead with hunger, saw a plump chicken by the side of the road and broke ranks to run after it. The commanding officer noticed and shouted 'Halt!' O' Riley ignored him and continued chasing the chicken. 'Halt I say!' screamed the officer, going red in the face. Finally O'Riley caught the chicken, and in front of the officer wrung its neck. 'There,' said O'Riley. 'That'll teach you to halt when the officer tells ye!'

Chemistry professor: What can you tell me about nitrates?
Student: They're cheaper than day rates.

A football manager was being interviewed after a match. 'I promised the lads we'd either win, lose, or draw, and I didn't let them down.'

'My wife and I have only argued once in ten years of marriage.'
'Remarkable.'

'Not really. See that scar?'

A vicar asked a man in his parish why he never attended church. 'Every time you go there somebody throws something on you,' said the man. Confused, the vicar asked what he meant. 'The first time you go they throw water on you, the second time they throw confetti on you, and the third time they throw earth on you.'

Two men were walking home late from the pub. 'What will you say to your wife?' asked one. 'Nothing,' replied the other. 'She usually thinks of something.'

Daughter: I want a husband who is easily pleased.
Mother: Don't worry dear. That's probably the kind you'll get.

She: Did you get a commission in the army?
He: No, just a basic salary.

'I see Jane's turned 35. When is she thinking of getting married?'
'Constantly.'

A burglar who is working too hard could do with arrest.
The British ambassador was to give an after- dinner speech in China. The room was full of Chinese politicians, none of whom

could speak English. Hoping to break the ice before his speech, he told a long joke. When he'd finished the interpreter said one sentence and everyone in the room burst into loud laughter. Afterwards the ambassador asked the interpreter how he'd managed to sum up the joke so briefly. 'I didn't,' he explained. 'I just said "the ambassador has just told a joke. Everybody please laugh."'

'They do argue over trifles but I'm not sure that's such a bad sign.'
'How so?'
'It may mean they don't have anything else to argue about.'

'You're not just marrying that man for his money, are you?'
'Of course not. It's the little things about him that I like.'
'Such as?'
'Oh, his little place in the country, his little flat in town, his little private island...'

'Darling, in this moonlight your teeth are like pearls.'
'Oh really – and since when have you been in the moonlight with Pearl?'

She: You remind me of the sea.
He: What? Wild, restless and romantic?
She: No, you make me sick.

A woman in a top floor flat dialled 999 and asked to speak to the fire brigade. 'My husband's gone out and locked my bedroom door, and now a man's trying to get in through my window,' she said, with a trembling voice. 'This is the fire brigade,' said the voice on the line. 'You need the police.' 'No I don't,' said the woman. 'You're the ones with the ladder.'

Little Johnny: We're getting another room put on our house.
Little Jimmy: That's nothing. I heard my dad say we're getting another mortgage on ours!

Intuition: the strange instinct that tells a woman she's right, whether she is or not.

It was amateur night at a Glasgow music hall and a pretentious poet, with anguished face, began to declaim a poem in a mournful voice from the stage. 'Alone, alone, all, all alone!'
'Aye,' shouted a heckler from the audience, 'and no bloody wonder!'

Wife: I'm looking at this chart from the doctor to find out if my height-to-weight ratio is correct.
Husband: And is it?
Wife: No – according to this I should be six inches taller.

Little Johnny was locked in his room. 'Now don't let me catch you stealing biscuits from the kitchen again,' said his mother. 'Well,' replied the boy tearfully 'I tried not to let you catch me this time.'

Vicar (collecting in the street): My mission is to save prostitutes.
Drunk: Tha's great rev'rend. Could yer save a couple for me too?

Man (to in-laws visiting): Is there anything I can get you? Tea? Coffee? Hats and coats?

Traveller (in railway buffet): Are these stale buns all you have to eat?
Bored waitress: I don't have to eat them – you do.

Prison visitor (to convict): Why are you here, my good man?
Convict: I'm the victim of unlucky number thirteen.
Prison visitor: How so?
Convict: Twelve jurors and a judge.

'I have a foolproof method to promote hair growth.'
'What's that?'
'Stop having it cut.'

Before marriage, men will swear undying love. After marriage, they just swear.

An agony aunt was asked by a young lady how to get rid of unwanted hair on the upper lip. 'Push the young man away' was the reply.

An Australian visitor to England was asked what he thought of Shakespeare. 'No idea, mate,' came the reply. 'I prefer Foster's beer.'

Nurse: Doctor, a patient has collapsed in the surgery and we can't get her back up.
Doctor: Well see if you can get any other part of her up!

Foreman: You know you're not supposed to smoke while you're working.
Labourer: Who says I'm working?

Mrs Jones had just got her driving licence and was proudly giving her non-driving friend Mrs Brown a lift. She stopped at a red light, took out her compact and powdered her nose. 'Shouldn't you be looking at the traffic light?' asked her friend. 'Oh I don't need to,' said Mrs Jones. 'I just listen for that loud tooting noise it makes.'

Alcohol: a liquid for preserving almost anything – except secrets.

A factory manager put a sign on the shop floor which read 'I want to see everyone happy at their work. Please write below any suggestions that will help bring this about.' The next day somebody had written beneath it: 'Wear noisy shoes.'

Husband: You ought to put something away for a rainy day.
Wife: I have.
Husband: Really – what?
Wife: An umbrella.

Mrs Smith: My husband buys me a new coat every time it's my birthday.
Mrs Jones: How lovely! You must have an awful lot of coats.

The bereaved relations gathered round to hear the solicitor read the will. 'Being of sound mind...I spent everything before I died.'

If every car in the world were placed end-to-end...it would be the M25.

'The government's told us we all need to tighten our belts. What are you going to do about it?'
'Wear braces.'

A man went into a junk shop and saw an amateurish landscape painting in an old frame. The picture was horrible, but looking more closely, the man noticed that the frame was hallmarked solid silver. 'How much for this old picture?' asked the man. 'Oh that,' said the shopkeeper, 'you can have that for two pounds.' With great excitement the man paid the money. 'The frame's not included
though,' said the shop keeper. 'That's ridiculous,' said the man. 'Why on earth can't I have the frame as well?' 'Because,' said the shopkeeper with a smile as he removed the picture, 'that frame's helped me sell 75 pictures.'

McPherson was known as the most parsimonious man in the whole of his small Highland town. One day the minister was out collecting for a new church hall. McPherson refused to donate. 'Everybody's given something but you,' said the minister.
Still the man would not be moved. Eventually inspiration struck the clergyman and he said 'Mr McPherson, if you donate just five pounds, I will display the bank note on the wall of the new hall, with the inscription 'donated by Angus McPherson'.
The canny Scot thought for a moment. 'So you're not going to spend the money, then?' 'No,' said the minister. 'It will be there in perpetuity as an example to all, of your Christian charity.' 'I'll do it,' said McPherson. 'But I'll give ye a cheque instead.'

Wife: I mended that hole in your jacket pocket for you dear. Aren't you pleased?
Husband: Yes...but how did you know there was a hole there?

A man attended his wife's funeral, and after the ceremony, the clergyman approached him and said 'My good man; I know that at this time you are sorely grieved; but always remember, there is one who will console you, who shares in your suffering, and who will enfold you in arms of unfailing love.' The man wiped away his tears and said 'That's good to know vicar...what's her name?'

Paterfamilias (about to punish son for lying): When I was your age, my boy, I never told a lie.
Son: What age did you start?

Woman to bank clerk: I wish to make a withdrawal from my husband's part of our joint account.

Molly: That Fred Smith is a terrible ladies' man.
Polly: Why's that?
Molly: Well he's asked me out three times, and I've turned him down every time – and now he's going out with someone else!

McNab invited McTavish over to his house for supper. To McTavish's disgust, McNab took the larger of the two herrings from the dish. 'I don't think much o' your manners,' said McTavish. 'If I'd been in your place I would have taken the smaller fish.' 'Well,' replied McNab, 'You've got it noo.'

Sunday school teacher (to class): Can anyone tell me what we must do before our sins are forgiven?
Little Johnny: Start sinning!

Mother (to son): If you promise not to say 'damn' I'll give you ten pence.
Little Johnny: Alright then. I know another word that's worth at least a pound!

McTavish won the lottery and was so shocked that he collapsed in a dead faint and was ordered to stay in bed by the doctor. His wife instead went to collect the money from the lottery office. The press had heard about the big win, and a reporter thrust a microphone at Mrs McTavish. 'What's the first thing your husband's going to do with the money?' he asked. 'Count it,' she replied.

'My dear McTavish, (said the clergyman) do ye not know that whisky kills more people than road accidents?'
'Maybe so minister, but personally I'd rather be drunk than run over.'

A politician was visiting a lunatic asylum. While being shown around by the supervisor, the visitor said 'That woman over there...is she dangerous?' Glancing towards the woman in question, the supervisor said 'some of the time, yes.' 'But she has such a vicious look about her,' replied the politican. 'Why is she allowed to walk around?' 'Can't help it,' said the supervisor. 'But isn't she under your control?' asked the politician. 'Not really,' replied the supervisor. 'She's my wife.'

Husband: Our little son was so pretty as a baby. But now he's getting uglier every day.'
Wife: Well you didn't expect him to resemble you straight away did you?

Woman (to cleaning lady): That jug you broke yesterday belonged to my great-great-grandmother.
Cleaning lady: Thank heavens for that! I was worried it might be new!

A man passed an old hardware shop called 'The Three Wonders.' Puzzled by what it could mean, he went into the cluttered interior and asked the shopkeeper where the shop's name came from. Without saying a word, the shopkeeper pointed to a sign above the counter:

You wonder if I have it.
I wonder where it is.
Everybody wonders how I find it.

Wife: What do you think of these new shoes? They were free.
Husband: Really? Why were they free?

Wife: Well, they were marked down from £80 to £40, so I bought them with the £40 I saved.

Policeman: Come quietly now. The magistrate will want to see you in the morning.
Prisoner: No he won't. He told me he never wanted to see me before him again.

'It isn't the £25,000 I have in the bank that makes you want to marry me, is it?' said the young woman to her suitor. 'It certainly isn't,' he replied. 'I thought it was much more than that.'

'My wife worships me. She places a burnt offering before me every night.'

Customer (in barber shop): I'd like my hair cut please.
Barber: Certainly sir. Any particular way?
Customer: Yes – off.

A woman saw a man in the street begging, with a sign round his neck which read 'deaf and dumb'. As she put some money in his cup, he said 'thank you.' 'I thought you were supposed to be deaf and dumb,' said the woman indignantly. 'I'm not, missus,' said the man. 'I'm just minding the spot for the bloke until he gets back.' 'Oh...alright then,' said the woman. 'But where's he gone?'

'He's over there in the pub,' said the man, 'listening to the juke box.'

Tiresome visitor: Do you know, whenever I hear Mozart, I am completely carried away.
Host: What a pity. Our record player is broken.

'I saw you the other night by the docks winking at a woman.'
'I wasn't winking. Something got in my eye.'
'She got in your car as well!'

'Did you hear the story about the two holes in the ground?'
'No.'
'Well, well.'

A Hollywood actor was boring his dinner party companion with tales of his great achievements. 'But enough about me,' said the actor, to the other's great relief. 'What did you think of my latest film?'

New post office worker (to old hand): This parcel is marked 'fragile'. What does that mean?
Old hand: Means only throw it underarm.

'I don't find my new girlfriend very attractive.'
'Why not?'
'In the first place, she's too fat...and she's too fat in the second place as well!'

Daughter: Do all turkeys have wishbones, mummy?
Mother: Yes dear.
Daughter: Then why don't they all wish that Christmas never comes?

McTavish took his wife to the theatre. They sat in the gallery and Mrs McTavish got so engrossed in the play that she leant too far over the rail and fell into the stalls below. 'Jeanie, Jeanie,' cried McTavish after her in anguish. 'For God's sake try to get up. It costs thirty pounds doon there!'

'How long was your last secretary with you?'
'She was never with me – she was against me from the start!'

'Everyone needs to breath oxygen to live. But it was only discovered in 1783,' said the science teacher. Little Johnny put up his hand. 'Please sir,' he asked, 'what did they breath before it was discovered?'

'That man in the pub kept trying to put his hand down my dress.'
'What did you say to him?'

'"Keep it up."'

What is a woman worth? Double you, O man.

Wife (to stingy husband): I don't like our new house.
Husband: Why not?
Wife: There are no curtains in the bathroom. The neighbours can see me taking a bath.
Husband: Why worry? They'll buy their own curtains soon enough!

The judge addressed the court in a sombre voice. 'I received in the post this morning a cheque for ten thousand pounds from the defendant and a cheque for fifteen thousand pounds from the plaintiff. This sort of thing will not be tolerated in my court. The case will be tried strictly on its merits. I have therefore arranged for five thousand pounds to be returned to the plaintiff.'

Fortune teller (to lady): Madam, your future looks black.
Lady: Wait a minute, I've still got my gloves on!

A tourist was visiting the Alps. A guide took him on a long, steep climb to the top of a mountain. 'Look down there,' said the guide. 'Isn't it beautiful down there in that valley?' 'If it's so beautiful down there,' said the tourist breathlessly, 'why the devil did you bring me all the way up here?'

A man went to a restaurant famous for its rude waiters. 'Give me two fried eggs, and a few kind words,' said the man. The waiter brought his order. 'What about the kind words?' said the man. The waiter leant over and whispered, 'Don't eat the eggs.'

Waiter (in fashionable restaurant): How did you find the beef, sir?
Diner: Oh, I just moved a potato, and there it was.

Woman (to shop assistant): Could you take that dress out of the window for me?
Assistant: Certainly madam. Would madam care to try it on?
Woman: No – I just hate seeing it every time I walk past.

McTavish asked for a pint of beer in a pub. The beer didn't fill the glass. 'That's short,' said McTavish. 'No, we just use bigger glasses,' said the barman. McTavish drank the lot in one go. 'That'll be three pounds,' said the barman. McTavish put three fifty pence pieces on the bar. 'Here, this is short,' said the barman. 'Naw,' replied McTavish. 'I just use bigger coins.'

Marriage: the only scientific example of an immovable object co-existing with an irresistable force.

Paddy and Seamus were on a building site arguing about who was the stronger. 'See that wheelbarrow there?' said Paddy. 'I'll bet I can push a load in there that you can't.' 'Go on and fetch it then,' said Seamus, 'and we'll see about that. There isn't a load in the world I can't shift.' Paddy brought the wheelbarrow over and put it in front of Seamus. 'Alright then,' said Paddy. 'Get in.'

Two elderly gentlemen were talking in their club. 'The other day I dreamt I was addressing the House of Lords,' said one, 'then I woke up – and realised I was!'

Two men were drinking at the club and a third walked in.
'Is that Timkins, the criminal lawyer?'
'Yes,– but nothing's been proven.'

'Daddy, I found this bikini lying on the beach.'
'Well done son. Now come with daddy and show me exactly where you found it.'

'Gambling has brought our family closer together.'
'How's that?'
'We've had to buy a smaller house.'

'I have a terrible time remembering people's names,' said Smith. 'So do I,' replied Jones, 'but I have a clever way of getting them to repeat it. I just ask "Do you spell your name with an e or an i?" It usually works.'

'I've tried that method before,' said Smith. 'It worked fine until I tried it with Mr Hill.'

'State the amount of coal exported from the United States in any one year,' was a question on the schoolboy's examination paper. He thought for a moment then wrote '1492: none.'

Jones' wife was in the delivery room of the hospital. Terrible groans and cries came from within. When she finally came out with their new baby, Jones said with tears in his eyes, 'my dear, I'm so sorry to have caused you this trouble!' 'Don't worry dear,' replied Mrs Jones. 'I'm sure it wasn't your fault.'

Sign in shop: 'Nothing sold for credit. Not much sold for cash, either.'

'And this, I suppose,' said a man in an art gallery, 'is one of those horrors you call modern art.' 'No sir,' replied the guide. 'That's just a mirror.'

She: When we're married, we ought to have no secrets. You must tell me everything.
He: But...er...I don't know everything!

Little Johnny went into a sweetshop and asked for a bag of jelly babies. 'But I want them all to be boy babies,' said Johnny with a serious expression. The shopkeeper smiled indulgently and asked why. 'More jelly on them,' replied Johnny.

McTavish met his wife at the station after a trip to London.
'Did ye bring me a present?' asked his wife.
'Aye, I did,' replied McTavish. 'I got ye a souvenir mug.'
'Whit does it say on it?'
'British Rail.'

Judge: Why didn't you attempt to settle this case out of court?
Defendant: That's just what we were doing your honour, until the police came and broke us up.

An American tourist was unimpressed by the masterpieces in the Louvre. 'We've got plenty of priceless paintings in the United States too,' he said. 'I know,' said the guide. 'Van Gogh painted 900 pictures, and America has all ten thousand of them.'

Some people like their work so much, they can just sit and look at it for hours.

At a highland wedding, one of the guests expressed surprise that the collection plate had been passed round during the service.

'Yes it is unusual,' said the church elder, 'but the father of the bride requested it.'

'An astrologer told me not to marry in January if I wanted to avoid trouble. Of course, the same advice holds good for the other eleven months too.'

'The pianist tonight was wonderful. I hear he learnt to play at four.'
'Four this afternoon?'

'I get the hardest part of the day's work done before breakfast.'
'Which part's that?'
'Getting up!'

A rose by any other name would smell as sweet.
A chrysanthemum by any other name would be easier to spell.

A toastmaster was calling out the names of guests as they arrived at a banquet. A prominent local tailor entered and the toastmaster asked his name. 'Don't you remember me?' said the tailor. 'I made your trousers.' 'Ah yes,' said the toastmaster, and solemnly announced: 'Major Trousers.'

Paddy and Seamus visited Rome and went into a bar for some refreshment. Paddy nudged Seamus. 'See that feller over there,' he said, pointing to an elderly gent in the corner, 'sure and I tink that's the Pope.'

'Don't be so stupid,' scoffed Seamus. 'What would the Pope be after doing in a place like this?' 'I'm sure it's him,' protested Paddy. 'Alright, let's ask him,' said Seamus.

They went over. 'Excuse me sir,' said Seamus, 'but we was wondering....' Immediately the man shouted at them in heavily accented English 'Go to hell and leave me alone, damn you!' The two Irishmen went back to their seats. 'What a shame,' said Paddy. 'Now we'll never know!'

First secretary: How's your new boss?
Second secretary: Not bad, but he's a bit narrow minded.
First secretary: How so?
Second secretary: He thinks words can only be spelled one way.

'You say the wedding went off without a hitch?'
'Yes – the chap due to be hitched didn't turn up.'

'I heard a great joke the other day. Perhaps I've told it to you?'
'Is it funny?'
'Yes.'
'Then you haven't.'

A young lothario entered an expensive boutique with his new girlfriend late one Friday afternoon. He told her she could have anything in the shop so she picked out a designer dress priced at £10,000. 'We can't take such a large amount right away, sir', said the assistant, 'but we will put the dress aside until Monday when your bank can confirm the payment.' On Monday the man received a phone call from the shop. 'I'm terribly sorry sir,' said the assistant, 'but the bank has declined the payment. They say you only have £50 in your account.' 'Oh I thought they probably would,' said the man, 'but thanks for a great weekend!'

The teacher wrote a sentence on the blackboard, which read: 'I didn't have no fun at the weekend.'
'Now children, how can I correct this?' she asked.
Little Johnny put up his hand. 'Get yourself a boyfriend, miss!'

A young couple filled their new home with products entirely paid for with coupons cut from cereal packets. They proudly showed their respective parents round the house, pointing out all the gadgets they'd bought. 'There are four rooms in this house and you've only shown us three,' said the woman's mother. 'What's in that other room?' 'Oh that,' replied her daughter. 'That's where we keep all the cereal packets.'

I'm not saying it's a small town, but if you see a girl out with a man old enough to be her father, he probably is.

'I could live on onions and garlic alone.'
'You'd have to.'

A man was travelling on a train from London to Edinburgh and noticed an elderly man in Highland dress get out at every station. Each time he ran madly along the platform, bought a ticket, dashed back and got into the train just in time.
After a while the man became curious, and asked the Scotsman what was going on. 'Weell,' he said, 'I dinnae want to pay for a ticket for the whole journey to Edinburgh.' 'Why on earth not?' asked the Londoner, suspecting foul play.
The Scot explained: 'I've just been told by the doctor I've a heart condition and could drop dead at any moment.'

Book keeping taught in one easy lesson: don't lend them.

23 year old Miss Jones was to be married to 50 year old Mr Brown. 'I'm not sure I understand these "May to December" marriages,' said her mother. 'I can see that he gets a beautiful young woman for "May" but what on earth is the attraction for you in "December"?' The bride to be smiled and replied, 'Christmas.'

There are two reasons why some people don't mind their own business. One is that they haven't any business, and the other is that they haven't any mind.

'Didn't I meet you in Swansea?'
'Don't think so I've never been to Swansea.'
'Neither have I. It must have been two other fellows.'

At a psychology conference three academics were discussing the topic of prenatal influence. 'When my mother was pregnant with me, she tripped over a dog, and consequently I have a terrible fear of dogs,' said one man.
'When my mother was pregnant with me, she almost fell from a bus; and I have a phobia about public transport,' said another.
'What nonsense,' said the third man. 'When my mother was pregnant with me she collapsed on top of a gramophone. But it didn't affect me...affect me...affect me...affect me...'

Wife: Did you see that lovely hat Mrs Jones was wearing at morning service today?
Husband: Er, no dear. I'm afraid I was asleep most of the time.
Wife: Well really, I don't know why you bother coming to church.

Biology teacher: Can anyone name the parts of the bowels?
Little Johnny: Yes miss. A, E, I, O, U.

Stable owner (to new jockey): Have you ever had an accident while riding?
Jockey: No, sir.
Owner: Then where did you get that scar on your head?

Jockey: Thrown from a horse, sir.
Owner: But you said you'd never had an accident.
Jockey: Yes sir. He did it on purpose.

At an elegant London ball a young lady and gentleman were dancing. 'They say I'm the best dancer in the country,' simpered the affected young female. 'You may be the best dancer in the country,' said the man, as his feet were trodden on yet again, 'but you don't seem to be when you're in town.'

Little Johnny was told by his teacher to write a full account of any cricket match he'd seen. The next day, the pedagogue was shocked to find just three words in Johnny's exercise book. 'Rain stopped play.'

'Waiter, what on earth is this you've just given me?'
'It's bean soup, sir.'
'I'm not interested in what it's been – I want to know what it is now!'

McTavish, a devout churchman, had never been to a race meeting before, but one day his friend McDougal persuaded him to go with him. He got McTavish to bet one pound on a horse which came in at 100-1. As the cashier paid out the money, McTavish said in astonishment to McDougal, 'Ye mean tae say I get all this for a poond? Jings man, how long has this been going on?!'

McDougal had a great idea for saving on cab fares. At Queen Street station he saw a man get in a taxi and heard him ask for a street close to his own. McDougal jumped in and sat on the seat next to him. 'Hello there,' said the canny Scot, holding out his hand in greeting. 'Mah name's McDougal.' 'Mine, sir,' replied the passenger, 'is not.'

'Dad warned me not to go to adult cinemas in case I saw something I shouldn't see there. He was right – I saw him.'

Wife: It says on this medical report you've fathered two children. But we've only got one.
Husband (nervously): Er – I think the other one was a secretarial error.

'How's it going with your new girlfriend?'
'She broke it off.'
'Better luck next time.'
'Yes...assuming the stitches hold.'

Made in the USA
Columbia, SC
15 November 2020

24590036R00050